A MAP OF RAIN DAYS

ESSENTIAL POETS SERIES 276

Canada Council
for the Arts

Conseil des Arts
du Canada

ONTARIO ARTS COUNCIL
CONSEIL DES ARTS DE L'ONTARIO

an Ontario government agency
un organisme du gouvernement de l'Ont

Canada

Guernica Editions Inc. acknowledges the support of the Canada Council for the Arts and the Ontario Arts Council. The Ontario Arts Council is an agency of the Government of Ontario.

We acknowledge the financial support of the Government of Canada.

JENNIFER HOSEIN

A MAP OF RAIN DAYS

GUERNICA
EDITIONS

TORONTO – CHICAGO – BUFFALO – LANCASTER (U.K.)
2020

Michael Mirolla, editor
Cover and interior design: Errol F. Richardson
Cover image: Jennifer Hosein
Interior images: Jennifer Hosein
Guernica Editions Inc.
287 Templemead Drive, Hamilton (ON), Canada L6M 2Z7
2250 Military Road, Tonawanda, N.Y. 14150-6000 U.S.A.
www.guernicaeditions.com

Distributors:
Independent Publishers Group (IPG)
600 North Pulaski Road, Chicago IL 60624
University of Toronto Press Distribution
5201 Dufferin Street, Toronto (ON), Canada M3H 5T8
Gazelle Book Services, White Cross Mills
High Town, Lancaster LA1 4XS U.K.

First edition.
Printed in Canada.

Legal Deposit – Third Quarter
Library of Congress Catalog Card Number: 2019949189
Library and Archives Canada Cataloguing in Publication
Title: A map of rain days / Jennifer Hosein.
Names: Hosein, Jennifer, author.
Series: Essential poets ; 276.
Description: Series statement: Essential poets series ; 276 | Poetry.
Identifiers: Canadiana 20190174722 | ISBN 9781771834414 (softcover)
Classification: LCC PS8615.O8225 M37 2020 | DDC C811/.6—dc23

In loving memory of my parents, Zalakha and Mubarak, and my dear friend Nik Beat

CONTENTS

I LOVE YOU

I Love You

       I love you
he said.
       You are my heart.

       I'll cut your tongue out
       so you can't speak
       like that
              anymore.

       I'll cut your feet off
       and I'll carry you around
              when I want.

       I'll cut your hands off
       so you can't touch
       another man's face
       the way
              you touch mine.

       Will you cut my cunt out
she asked,
       so I can't fuck
       another man
              or even myself?

       I'll cut it out
       and I'll keep it
              in a locked drawer.

I'll take it out
when I need to
and place it
in the space
            between your legs.

Or, maybe,
if I'm angry
I'll take it into another room
put it around my cock
            and thrash around some.

I'll cut your breasts off
so no man
can look at them.

Then
you can wear
            what you like.

            What will you leave me?
she asked.

I'll leave you my right hand
to hold
when you're alone
and I'll leave you
            my heart.

Winter

(for my mother, Zalakha, and my daughter, Natasha)

I am Demeter
     in winter
     black as Hades
turning fields to stone
forests to dust
in my wrath and despair
that my beloved
        is gone

I pick rocks
     from the side
     of the road
to eat in the absence of corn
They thunder
along my intestines
dulling the noise
       in my head

I scream
     inside the walls
     of February
wait for my beloved
who is light, breath, sun, spring
make love to boys
I have turned to bones
in this drought
       I have brought

I am Persephone
        bound
        beneath the light
longing for the tick
of my mother's heart
the pad of her yellowed feet
                on the floor

But my winter
        will linger
        for years
and my mother will tread
across the skies
her feet into mountains
her face yellow as the sun
peering down at the shadow
              I have become

Demeter
        is my mother
Persephone
        my daughter
I am neither
I am all
I am only winter

Heart

My mother's heart
begins to drift away
but we are selfish
and tell her
to let them fix it
and we pace
and pace the days
Don't tell her
it's a porcine
aortic valve's
open and close
that keeps her
herself
until she is not
herself:
voice crooked
face fallen
buttons askew
and pants
half on the floor
I cannot begin
Beloved mother is a
clipped-winged bird that
floats around in lace-
edged nightgowns
soft, soft skin
like a schoolgirl's
shooing away
the cats and always
packing her clothes
to go home

A Map of Rain Days

I am bent by the way
that these things go

Put my face in my hands
and pull the skin taut
across miles and miles

Walk down the corridors
in my mother's bruised shoes

My mother's toes are
crooked and curled

in a misguided, arthritic map
of rain days

Valentine's Day

This boy
folds his head into walls
bites his own head off
turns the day to tatters.

Snow traces wedding lace
on window panes
caresses a man who struggles
with his foolproof design
for suicide
so foolproof that his friends
finding him so
cannot tell how he did it.
Third time a charm.

Mother, grandmother, sister
punches buttons on the telephone.
Her sister says, *Don't call
bothering people all the time,*
but she calls everyone she can think of
and strangers, too
cries on the daughter's voicemail,
I'm so unhappy here,
sits alone in a corner, by choice
if that's what you can call it
these days, and her hands shake
all the time.

The Scarborough Bluffs

Summer swelter turns to breeze
and dusk swells, smears the windshield
purple, so I turn up the radio and drive us
to the lake where families

are spread thick on rocks:
Arabic rap thuds, toddlers wail
while white sand bluffs tower over great-
aunts tugging babies along the pebbled paths

We lean our ears into the lake lapping
my mother and I holding hands
as if time had reversed
then one last stop to gawk at the bluffs

Waiting

My mother
stands at the window
looking out
at the cars below

while the days
go around in circles
and Tuesday
is April
is another year gone by.

Her voice is careful
and ragged
catching on air.

She calls all day
every day
asking why
I haven't called.

I call. Every day
we find words
to hand to each other
like gifts.

She leaves messages
breathless words
thrown out
to latch onto love.

My brother
has no time
for the heart-breakingness
of the old

and I have no place left
to put the sorrow
she hands me.

January

Tomorrow is my daughter's birthday.
I promised her a cake before midnight
and I do everything I can to stop the car
from turning me back home, my heart pounding
against the steering wheel.
But my mother is waiting by the window
and she doesn't know, and then she does
tossing fragments of her old life
into plastic bags: a handful of photographs,
a miscellany of yellowed papers,
too-tight clothes, and slippers.
I wish we could go back:
to the doctors' waiting rooms,
Chinese supermarkets, mango popsicles,
and the lake. Then, I felt caged, but now
it's all I want. I take her socks off,
pull a nightgown over her head,
kiss her and hug her and tuck her
into the cold, stinking night.

I race down the Don Valley Parkway
towards January 6th, but there is a car
rolled over on the highway.
I run in the door at five minutes to midnight
and put candles on the cake.

Love fills me up like a balloon,
so full and stretched and thin am I.

Breath

Our breath sits heavy
on the dashboard,
Mother floats around the car
with the snow. Our boots crunch
and slide across new graves, and Uncle says,
She is here, No, she is here,
blowing his vodka breath into the sky.

Feathers

Only feathers
string me up across the sky
one nudge or wrinkle
and I fall
crash through violet dusk
and skyscrapers
and land
this wingless
landlocked
flattened creature of despair

Conductor

Take my hand
tonight
on the snow white
tracks
of my dreams.
Be my night
conductor and
steer me
from the monsters
that throw me
up against the walls
of this box car life.

Wheel

Night batters
      at my skin
pushes
      into me
heaves
      against my ribs
propels me
      onto haggard streets.
I cry
      please
but you cannot hear
      the words
jammed in my throat
      like some old rag.
I bounce
      on the road,
this night creature stretching
      my bones
into a wheel
      that bends
and breaks me
      all the night long.

Wedding Day

(for Natasha)

You are the princess
beneath my pillow

I am the pea that sways
in the corners of your night

You are my map of the city
Every place

is only meaningful in the way
that you were there with me

This is the airport
that you are leaving me from

This is the road
that takes me away from you

When you leave
you take the light away

I wait
for your whisper

hold tight to the pillow
that you laid your head upon

as if it were love
itself

pull stitches
out of your discarded dresses

unravelling
the years between us

Then, I begin to sew
your wedding dress

Tree lights
string me across the desert

my feet
parched with longing

Across the universe
in a sun-bleached room

I lay the snow-white dress
on the bed

Today
is your wedding day

You tug at the hem of your dress
dip your white heels into the grass

in the Hollywood afternoon
You are breathtakingly happy

In the morning
I have to return to my *life without you*

I press my tears to the door
of your hotel room to feel your breath

When I look for you in mirrors
you shine behind my eyes

Sometimes you whisper to me
to wrap you tight

in the star-punched
night

Swish

These days
she lives with a man
on a long stretch of grass
between Mennonite farms

Wind turbines *Swish Swish*
in the wet snow

A horse and buggy
grow faint beneath
the white laden trees
that bend across the road

Dogs bark
at the surprise of guests
on such a forlorn day

And your girl waits
on the other side
of the glass door
snow already piled on the porch

Dead Boys

Ghosts
of dead boys
      scatter
on your balcony
      peer in and
      laugh
at your woes
      tell you,
Wait,

but you stink of life
and piss-sweat
as you drag around
the streets and back
through half-dead hours.

You cry in your bed
and wake at three a.m.
eyes bright and expectant.

Wait,
      the boys whisper
as you tiptoe
through the halls.

Look,
      they say.
Kiss that boy.

Window

She rolled through sky
like butter

night effervescent
with the glow that spit out of her

embers turning into stars in the sky
that could not love her the way she,
or anybody, needed

But you
loved her

gave her walls
to keep her safe
food to buy her time
but the walls bent

as if your sins had chewed
furiously at them

multi-legged termite ghosts
through days and days

And what did she see
when she stepped into sky
and dreams
and dusk
that sounded like city squalor
banging prayers
in her head?

And how can you sleep
in your bed
by the window
that I
in another spring
leaned out of to watch
the schoolboys below?

Fog

If she had leaned
into a night such as this,
fog clotted thick as cream
across rooftops,
would she have paused
and rested in a cloud
before she touched ground,
this beautiful, fallen angel?

Pacific

Fragments of her shadow
cling to the sky,
minuscule pieces like ash
flung by man in the moon wrist.
When you swim
with her ashes in the Pacific,
her kiss tucks you back
into the swirling ruckus
she left behind.

Milk

I see your loss
staggering across the sky
like milk in June
curdled and warm.
Your eyes unwind
in threads of rage
across the room,
knocking down the glass
which you step through
on your way
out of winter.

EXILE

Mon Pays

My country
is an ice storm
trees bent to the devil
and smelly
damp boots.

On the bus, our noses
are the same matching red
toques pulled low
over foggy, crisp breath
holes in our glove-thumbs

yet he scowls and says,
Go home, Go back
to your country
where you came from.

So I tell him,
Yes, I'll go back
to the foot of Mount Royal
to the unconditional arms
of my mother
wrapped around me
and my smelly boots.

I tell him
my mother's black coat
against the winter-white *paysage*
is always
and only home
and he
should be so lucky.

White

(after the U.S. election, November 8, 2016)

I used to daydream
that White
was a tablet
you could place
on your tongue
and the morning
would be a better place.
But here, now
in my tiny radius
of the world
I am almost white;
I pass through doors
and no one sees me
or calls me names
to my face.
But it's only here
that I pass
in perfectly pressed clothes
that I nip and tuck
to not draw attention
to my skin.

Not north
where I am a dark spot
on snow.
Not south
where I am a stain
that warrants walls
to keep me out
registries

bullets
and jails.
The other day
it occurred to me
that I didn't wish
to be white
anymore
the way I had wished
when I was ten
and seven
and five
the first time I was
punched
spit on
pushed
barred
called *Paki*
and Go back
to your Country
and
You don't
belong.
That was a long time
ago, when I couldn't walk
with my head up
or down.

But
yesterday
they put a noose
around a boy's neck
and yanked
and they are yelling
Go back
to where you came from
and *Your time's up*
and *Heil Hitler.*

I think
I might need that pill
soon!

Exile. Canadian Shield

In the city, I cannot stop.
In the Canadian Shield
there is stillness.
Windows and sky.
Aunty cannot bear
to live in this faraway place
while Uncle is thinning
out of the living world.
They hide in the basement
as if they are hidden in rock
and snow.
Aunty moved into my bedroom
when I was two.
She slipped the fear
out of the night
when she entered the room.
On her wedding day
I danced in the front yard
drunk on cheap something
stomping snow, marveling
at the moon and the whoosh
in my head.
I see their footprints
getting smaller in the snow
but it is summer, and the rain
has birthed a fog of mosquitoes.

Unfamiliar

I lie awake conjuring cane
and saltwater sea.
I wish I had asked.
Tell me about my skin.
I used to wish to fade into sky.
How did my father learn
to put his feet down
on unfamiliar soil?

My mother's steps
had a ring to them of
certainty. She knew.
I did not.

Rain on the Island

Rain on the island
erases the fences
we put up on the landscapes
we have become:
tributaries of loss and
shadows of longing
are mapped on our torsos
until we are criss-crossed
and unrecognizable
Against the impending storm
farmers have wrapped their bales
in a funereal white that shimmers
like water on the lake

Espanola

Long trucks
are full of skeletons
at dusk,
and the sun
is a vermilion afterthought,
the sky bent into grids
of power lines
while lonesome birds
line up at the gate
to heaven,
just 49 kilometres
from Espanola.

HAMMERSMITH & QUEEN

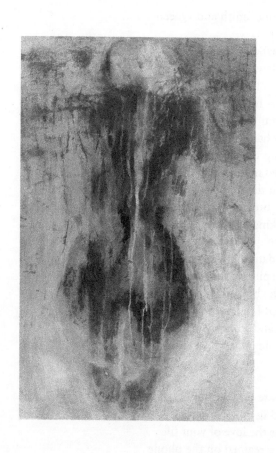

Hammersmith & Queen

1.
Hammersmith and Queen
two a.m.
my parked car
windows down.
I reach through the night
to rest my fingers
in your uncombed
dirty hair,
roll up the windows
as two men weave
down the street towards us,
their broken, bird-like swagger
breaking us apart.
I turn on the radio
and dance you outside my car.
You spin me around
on the broken boardwalk.
When I pause to wipe
the sand from my eyes,
you are gone.

2.
You are on your porch
looking out at the boardwalk.
I was the love of your life
you screamed on the phone
once, twice, many times
many years ago.

I used to sit in my parked car
in your driveway
after I had run out the door,
leaving you behind
with your beer
and one hundred empties
tucked away beneath the sink
with your bad dreams.

3.
Your apartment
has smelled of cat
since she died and left you
and her cat behind
to fill the black
soulless nights.
You invite your friends
one by one
or all at once
to keep you company
because you cannot fill the space
she left in your bed.
The cat is pale-hued and jumps
through the window
like a ghost.

4.
As I fly down Lakeshore Boulevard
in my car, Jack is dying.

His wife bends over him,
children askew
in the darkened room.
I cannot sleep tonight.
While I kill time
until the pink sky comes
to kiss me to sleep,
two blocks away,
Jack dies.

Ink

In the mornings
my fingers were stained
the colour of the ink
that I used
to write you into my dreams.

Sometimes you were black
ink handprints along the walls.
All the colours that I used
to paint you
were propped up around my life,
blocking the real
and putting into its place
a semblance of you.

By the spring
I had so many canvasses
that you began to appear
as a man
breathing and soft-mouthed
reclining on my bed.
I could not tell real
from writing
skin from paint.

Whip-Poor-Will's Song

You erase yourself like words from a blackboard.
Days roll, and I long up and down the avenues.

You fold nights into napkins that I fill my pockets with.
How hard I toil to turn them into stories

to savour and pine for. Bent over you
I become the stillness of night, the snow itself.

I worship the winter that holds you to my breath,
croon a whip-poor-will's song,

see you come and go, spinning circles
around days between then and then.

Road

I open for you on the road
fill my car up with wet longing.
Pinch me, bend me, let me
suck you up with my hands
swallow you with my eyes
yearn with my tongue up and
down the twisted night.
I am so far from home
on this road that winds and
bends through snow and stars
how will I find my way back?

Stories

The taste of you
stays on my tongue
like old pennies
while you dream
the sleep of angels.
I trace your face
into the night
on my ragged fingertips,
taste your breath
that spills stories
onto the sheets,
reach into your dreams
to put myself there.

Monsters

Morning
you turn and
I toss

I push along
the length of you

press my breath
and dust and dirt
into you

squeeze into you and
walk as far as I can
with you

far from the madness
of my bed
I fill you up with me and
you don't know

how my eyes
peer out of you
all the day long

and when you lay you
down to sleep, the monsters
come find me

and pull me back
to the hollow of my bed,
my mouth set in a jagged "O".

Fall

The leaves have fallen
from their hosts,
the way I fell from you.
Once you were air,
then you were cinders
that I spat up now
and then.

Samson

You were Samson to my Delilah
for just one night, kissed me
all night long as I'd heard
in the song on the radio
that burned my ears
on the lonely road day in, day out.

Be careful what you wish for:
the nights are long, so long
when someone touches you
and squeezes you and bends you
and breaks you, just so.

The leaves were careening
down to earth like drunken sailors
and I was looking for someone
to love me through the bone-
breaking dull of winter.

I did not think to summer
when you could snap your fingers
and there it would be
something looking like love.

I did not know you would be
Delilah to my Samson
tie me with bowstrings
tie me with ropes, capsize me
with a flick of your wrist

but when you put me
up against the wall by the door
and kissed me up and down
and your hair fell
into your ice-coloured eyes

it was like love songs
all night long as the stars
fell from the sky.

Spark

How I loved you
as I flew across the metropolis

to fall at your door
turn the key
creep into your bed

I rubbed the sleep
from your eyes
you turned me to the wall

that's how we loved
through the winter and spring
before you lost your home
so I took you in
and you took me over
the way a spark
consumes a forest

turned me to ash that stuck
to the soles of your feet
during your tirades
and blackouts

splattered your fabulous dinners
across the kitchen walls

banged on the bedroom door
while your son pleaded
Daddy, please

Leap Day

Leap day
is snow
blowing across your eyelids
when you finally kiss sleep
like a dead man
at eight in the morning

The telephone
begins ringing at ten
but you hear only
the snow falling
The wind
blows a storm through your eyes
the sky sits behind the clouds
and a storm
blows through again

For a few hours
I can live in the solace
of your sadness
because you can see who I am
in the moments
you are still

But I am always anticipating
the moment you throw your limbs
around the room
scattering your shattered soul
throwing your ugliest voice
at me

When your words knock me
to the floor
I pick up the pieces
and walk away
You watch the hours
drop like days through the night
walk in circles until nothing
just snow
and the dream of beer

So up again
to pull a bottle
from under the sink
like a magician pulling a rabbit
from a hat

Beer is your bread
your fish
your salvation

Song

(for Nik Beat)

I woke to you standing
by the foot of my bed
your song unfurling on my tongue
the exquisite words that could
cut the night in pieces
falling flat in the absence of you.
And each day hurts
like new, tight shoes
that will never be familiar
so I slip my arms through the sleeves
of the thrift store jacket
you wore to all the parties
a long-tressed girl on one arm
or both.
And once upon a time ago
it was me you picked up
in your car, rose petals crushed
into the floor and
Coke cans scattered everywhere.
And once, we stayed up all night
writing alongside the lapping
of the waves.
I look for you in shoeboxes
full of photographs
and around every corner
but I can't find you.
I miss the smell of you.
You didn't like to leave
your shoes by the door
baring the holes in your socks.

And I never finished the paintings
that I started of you.
The nights you sat, and I
painted, you talked about this girl
or that one, and I leaned into the dark
trying to find your face.

I still have a can of Diet Coke
that I am keeping for the next time
you stop by.

Constellations

Your ashes flung across the sky
form many constellations
over the lake. As we turn towards
our lives without you,
you linger, a ghostly-pale angel
made of dust,
dust to ashes lapping
against the shore.
Are you content
in the cosmos,
dancing until dawn,
Marilyn Monroe on one arm
and Linda on the other?

Maybe you don't want us
to leave you behind
in the frigid waters,
but we do,
holding our faces in our hands
so they don't crumble
into the sand,
grasping at each other
for misguided guidance.
Then we all run into the night
candles blown
songs sung
wishes tossed into the lake.
Before midnight
the alley by your window
is piled with the miscellany
of your life.

I have your clock,
still tick-tocking,
a record of your heart beat
for always and ever.
And I have your ashes
up my sleeves,
where I rubbed my hands
to keep you close, always.

Thieves

Across a landscape
of falling thieves
I spread my webbed fingers
sticky with child's tears.
Beneath the skin
porcelain armies thump and beat
against the windows
begging to fall into dawn
as angels.

ROMANCE

Romance

I tell you
I am not a romantic.
You say
I like to speak of the stars.
The stars fell.
The romance has been chewed
out of me
kisses carved away
so many things in
and out of me
I cannot tell my skin
from the floor
or the chill night air.

Voice

I attempt to trace
your tangled voice
in the black air
with the sandpaper
lips of my fingers
but my fingertips are just
garbled whispers

Skin

I write myself on your skin.
The night is all grey sky
streets damp with the tears of angels.
But your skin is air, and
I turn and toss in my bed
legs wrapped around the shadows.

Crow's Feet

Inked on my face
are shadows that you left
behind, imprints
of your lovers' hands
slapped across my face
tugging at my crow's feet
in the morning

Mouth

I reach
into the back
of my mouth
to pull pieces of you
out. But they stick
so I choke and fumble
through the days
after you are gone.

Ebb

There are moons
in your eyes
as you watch me
walking out the door.
I shiver with the ebb
and flow of your tears,
taste all of your bygones
in the words that follow me
through the sliver of light
I leave behind
when I close the door.

The City

I walked the city, glassy-
eyed. Pulled lovers out of hats
to ease the nights that twisted
sorrow like shoelaces.
The city pinned me
beneath its dirty jack boots.
Too-bright days
hurt my eyes to behold.

Cacophony

Huddle in a shadow
against the hard crack
and snap of winter.
Listen to your breath fall
and the cacophony of sheets
against our skin.

Between

In the night
twisted images bend
and shape me.
I sit up all night
examining the space
between us.

Weekend

For you I spread my
legs, and the sun came in

You opened my skin
like slicing a peach

The naked, sand-crusted soles
of my feet pressed into the dashboard
of the rented car

We were driving up
the three-hundred kilometre coast
of the bay

While I slept, your fingers
climbed through me

your eyes on the road
your hand caressing my turmoil

You tugged on my
slippery heart

November

November is a painting that we step into
falling head over heels into scarlet

laughter on our faces, though our hearts
are heavy with the mundane

But, driving home across the luminous landscape
Indian summer haze across the lake

and feet restless for sandals
I conjure you in my passenger seat

as the wind turns my hair into a whorl
and then what more is there that I can want?

HISTORY

History

Look at me
on his bed.
History
will not untie me.
His story, always his
story. Someone's his
story. His cock dances around
me. His cock like a beacon.
A game of sticks.
I tire
of the ins and outs
of me, my beauty
laid flat on the bed
for his story to unwind
the night, the morning,
the clothes from my back.
I am just un-
dressed.
No lace, no red,
no perfume, just
my skin
is me.

Used To

Sex
used to be

everything

to me
the much of it
the lack of it
the colours
that fled across
the back of my eyes

Pressed
into black night

flecks of damp

across
the backs of thighs
dip-dancing me
in a silent room
to the ruckus
in my head

I put
myself

in terrible corners

to feel
that slap-tumble
through dead-end days

Men put me
in a box
                or a bag
or an envelope
        but the stick
        always loosened
        and I fell out
                thump
onto the days

Subterfuge

I, too,
once lived a life of subterfuge
voice pressed into the phone
shoulder tucked into a wall
so that I became the thin voice itself
and little more

I know the moment of falling
flat onto the eggshells
that litter your house

You tiptoe, until one day
feet press into air
and you are ascending

I used to walk through clouds
climb painstakingly out of my skin
turning my back on the breathing life
that tied me down and
bound me up in electrical cords

Walls

I pulled your walls away
with my tongue

We lay inside each other
while the sky turned

I ran my fingers along your
face ribs thighs

seeking an opening
or even an exit

We feigned sleep, but
all night long we waited

still, inside each other
not a word

Cabin

I would keep you here always
suspended from the wall

good log walls
that would hold your weight

feather-weight bones
I could hold in my hands

the feel of you all around me
in the night

I would cook your meals
on the wood stove

that warms you through the day
spoon-feed you

wash your hands and feet
wrap my arms around you

keep your bones beneath my pillow
keep your bones

Break

Measure us
in food and skin
blood on the onions
bruises on our limbs
I watch you with eyes
planted on the ceiling
in a corner
beneath the bed

You have bayonets
for hands
that bend and break
the night

Velvet

Two nights
before I was to marry
the hawk-nosed madman
you appeared
russet-haired boy-man
let me lean into your bear's back
let me drink from you until dawn.
I woke to the telephone's cacophony
sun burning through the slats
pondered the marriage license on the table
and my daughter's gleaming hair
as I went out the door.
But you appeared again
tall as a carpenter
sleek as a boy
flesh and blood in Yvonne's kitchen
a glint in your green eye.
So we drank
and children ran in the house.
I prayed to a God I did not believe in
that the night would not end
that you would not leave us on the street
driving off in your white van.
But you did
so I put my daughter to bed
and answered the telephone
that had been ringing
and ringing. The madman
called me names
accused me of this and that.

I put my daughter in the stroller
and walked like the wind
to the bar where you were drinking
in a red velvet booth
on the second floor.
We lay my sleeping daughter
on velvet
like a princess on a pea
and I put on
my best funny and charming
until closing time
wishing you would take us home.
You took us to your house
beside the railway tracks
and I put my daughter to sleep in your bed.
A train raised the dead as it rolled by.
You went to sleep in the living room.
Of course
I eased myself out of your bed
careful not to wake the child.
You were sitting by the window
listening for trains.
We smoked a little
and I told you my tales
until you sent me to your bed
alone.
I went home in the morning
answered the phone
listened to the madman's
mad tales:

father dying
I love you
blah blah.
He lied, boldfaced.
You did not save me, bear-man
after all.
I saw you on the street
in the fall.
I was with my husband
and my daughter
bruises buried beneath a crooked smile.
You flashed your green eyes at me
and you were gone.

King of the Night

Like you
he chose me from afar

I had only seen a blurred face
a speeding car

but I knew his eyes
that followed me:

silver slits
opening the sky

Red is the colour of the night
when he comes, when I twist and run

and when I see his silver slit-eyes
breaking through the alleyways

I tear away, and when I am safe
behind locked doors

I turn around to find him:
in his hands he holds all of me

Travels

The sky gives off the sweet odour of chocolate. I am bathed in a downpour of Nestlé chocolate and still thinking of you. I cannot erase the years or your voice from my answering machine. You surround me.

From the window of the Don Mills 25 bus, the valley opens up like a womb in the rain.

I carry you around in the hollow of my chest. Beneath my ribs, you dig tunnels, hundreds of tunnels, and you won't leave.

For every step forward, I take two steps back, always towards you.

No one knows why I stay. Why you're back.

You make a mask for your face with your brittle anger. If I walked off this bus onto the frozen field, the field would become a lake, its crisp, translucent surface cracking and drawing me in.

The bleak caress of snow. Your cool hands in a circle around my neck. The apartment is as cold as frozen fields. My limbs sculpt snow angels in the sheets. You bring ice into the room.

Snow Days

Winter has come again and I am walking through the snowy fields of all the years I have left behind. Here, snow doesn't accumulate and children don't jump off balconies into snow higher than their hats. Winter in Montreal was Snow Days: snow forts and igloos, snow angels in a crisp white world. Now, my daughter makes snow angels on the floor of our apartment, sweeping her coat sleeve snow angel wings across the parquet floor. The last time I made snow angels was beside the St. Lawrence River: midnight, minus 20°, he followed at a distance, in his car, waiting for the blue and white *Service de Police* cruiser to leave. I left bloody lip prints beside the St. Lawrence River and bathed my bruises in the fresh snow.

Fists

I carry around anger and resistance in the palms of my hand, I said.

He pried open my fists, finger by finger. He moved in, knocking down all opposition. The palms of my hands, he saw, were empty. Behind his eyes, the hangman raged. Pushed my fingers backward until I thought I was fingerless, hoofed like a horse. He began to retreat, sickened by the coolness that surrounded me.

He dragged me through a hundred houses, a thousand streets. Across an ocean and a sea.

I tried to remember love and the sky before it rained.

Poison-Drunk

Pools of blood
scar the smooth surface
of the floor.

I weave spaces
through the walls
with my ugly wrist

watch the shadows
darken, listen for the jingle-
jangle of keys at the door

train my eyes to catch
the movement of poison-
drunk cockroaches on the walls

not the flicker of light
from headlights, not my own
shadow bending in slow-motion.

Words separate me
from you. You say,
Believe me it won't hurt.

I never believe you.
I sit up awaiting
betrayal.

Vessel

My soul collapses
      within its vessel
of bones
      and lies
at my feet
      discarded
like a shadow
      shattered
by the rain

OUBLIETTE

Oubliette

(An oubliette is a secret dungeon with a trap door, from the French, oublier, *to forget.)*

She put him in the oubliette and locked it. He paced and brooded about his love for her. He waited, but she did not come. He spat out his love for her and collected it in the yellowed palms of his hands. Soon it began to spill over and collect at his feet. Still she did not come. She brought him only wine and left it while he was sleeping. He did not eat. He drank the wine and became thirsty and bewildered. Bewilderment turned to dullness. Finally she came, to collect his love, but he had turned to dust.

The Dance

My heart is breaking
as the dancers lift my soul
up through their winding
fingers. Dreams beat
in my hollow chest.

Moon

Pieces of crescent moon
hold the night
like shards of glass
pressed to my head

Storm

      I am waiting for my love
he is coming for me through snow
outside is a storm
slow whispers in the still longhouse
      I am waiting for my love
shadows string across the ceiling
push across the wind
bend beneath the white-heavy sky
      I am waiting for my love
his eyes are webbed with mist and ice
I wrap my skin around the night
ice spreads up through trees
      I am waiting for my love
I can taste my love's blue skin
my heart jumping and still
I spread us out on hard ground
      I am waiting for my love

The Tattoo Woman

The tattoo woman
lies in her room and waits,
the tools of her trade
all around. When you enter,
her eyes tremble
beneath translucent lids,
her hands run down
all of you, you can feel
her heart beating
through her fingertips.
Her eyes wide and dark,
she takes you in,
speaks to you in tongues.

Widow

I did not want a husband
I wanted
        a tree
        a forest
        a black-winged crow
        black night and
                blue earth
        a bed of rocks
I wanted
        an ancient man-boy
                salt-eyed and ragged
I wanted
        fingertips for eyes
But now I am old
a faithless widow
        soft boys filling the spaces
                that rain cannot

After the Fire at the Asylum

(Buffalo, N.Y., 1800s)

Only the burnt-out shell
was left. The windows
were barred, and from between
the cold iron bars came wailing
and weeping, centuries old.
The broken feet of women
dragged across the wooden beams.
The men's shaved heads
were cool and dry.

Atlantic Crossing

She was my child-bride
my very breath.

We had planned it all
so well

her sixty inches folded and
stuffed and passed from hand to

hand and how could I not
have known?

Her protected and pampered
skin bruised and broken

and when I opened the suitcase
I heard her gasp

her quiet mid-Atlantic scream.
I saw her blue-faced beauty etched

upon my nights. O voyage
to freedom. O America.

Angolan Dance

(circa 1980s)

The dance began at dusk.
Thin brown shadows frolicked
on the walls of the huts.

Two hundred dancers swayed
in the torch-circle, oiled and wet.
Beads of sweat like God's tears.

Drums, and somewhere a radio blared.
The dancers' eyes were star-gazing.
Those who had two legs jumped up

and carried the dance. Most, however,
had wooden legs made in the factory
in town; these hobbled and

swung their arms about. Children
sat cross-legged on the ground. Some
danced boy-girl, or singly, stiffly

imitating the adults. Only the babies
could truly dance, their oiled bodies
glowing, untaught, free.

STREETS

Rapt

The promise of youth
flush with excitement

Live on the edge
of suicide

You have no vision
of the carcass of youth

that lies ahead
the swill and gore of it

But you lock
your bedroom door and

sit rapt on the bed holding
grief in your palms

1977

I.
blend into trees
     and sky
         in brown skin
stay tight to
     tree bark
hold your breath
         between the crisp steps
         of teenagers
     slipping past in a cloud
shed the cloak of trees
veer towards home
         where your thick socks
shuffle on the parquet floor

II.
     school
is black terror
so you walk into books
         like Alice
     blue jeans
     and tight skin
         hallucinogens
         and hatred
spun in webs
         through the hallowed halls

III.
you walk a thin gauntlet
     alone

Streets

The mean streets of the suburbs
when I was fifteen

were as ugly as sin to me
and I was as ugly

as the mythical monster
the brown-hued devil

that lived beneath the bridge
Sticks and stones broke all of me

as the townspeople called to arms
spit and rocks, and fists

They fanned away from the dark shadow
that spilled out of me like blood

So I ate only apples
and turned to bones
and my hair gleamed
and my eyes were hollow

as I crawled through the halls of the high school
hid in the bathroom stall

slid home quick through the afternoon
died in the night

Him

The stink of his
breath, fat hands
at my throat

I leaned back
into earth and
fell into barren sky

on a Baptist church lawn
near the bus stop.

Face

All the days
and all the shadows
     that I hid in
          so that I would not be seen
     yet
I was always dark
     concrete
          a blood-spot
on a crisp
     white shirt

They tried to
     scrub me
          wipe me
cut me out
Every day
it took an army
     of pains
          to prepare a face
     to confront the world.

I took my supplies
from the department store:
     books
          mascara
     a palette of shadows
buried in my pockets
     and crevices

They did not find the lipsticks
tucked into my closet
       with the monsters
              that paraded around my room
       all the night long
stripes of cerulean
       where their eyes would have been
              crimson lipstick
in place of the mouths
       they did not have
I had no mouth
to speak with, either
       I wanted to paint one
              on my mute face
       with the lipstick
I'd buried in the closet
       but
              the closet stank
of the monsters' revelry
       and I was banned
              from the department store.
So
I shut
       what was in the place
              of my mouth
       forgoing words
and food
       and love

Home

Home is the painter
you are the paint
                   splattered on days

Home is everything and
everything is
                   the company you keep

Famiglia holds you
to its bosom or spits you out
                   onto streets

Boys lean into street corners
reach into your dreams
                   put their hands there

Your black hair is a rope
of wind
                   behind you.

Summer drips furiously
so you wrap the cool lake around you
                   like a shawl

Boys splash and break
the sunlit lake
                   like shattering glass
Streets
burn the soles
                   of your sneakers

You trail behind your pack of girls
boys line the wall holding up brick
                    and mortar

Lean into a boy in a stairwell
as he drips down your skin with tongue
                    and sweat

1970

Before the tanks rolled in
we rode everywhere
in a posse

Down the mountain
on *Rue Victoria*
dragging our feet

to slow our bikes
on the steep incline
burning the soles

of our sandals
slipping and sliding on our
neon-yellow banana seats

When the tanks rolled in
we worried
when they cancelled

Halloween, running
to every house we could get to
before curfew

Light

You are a tiny girl in a third-floor walk-up
scattering your doldrums here and there
following your mother's ponytail as she walks out of rooms
always left behind to struggle with unspoken monsters
or a pall of dullness.

The city seethes outside the tall windows
you toss and battle through the night
with the demons that accumulate in piles around the
          painted bed
that locks you in with a snap but never
locks them out

Black seeps between the bars when your mother
paints the room with a flick of a switch
she brushes the room dead-dark with you in the middle
dark as a hole in the night that starts in your little clenched
          fist and goes
until the end of time.

Yet still you reach for the sliver of light
she leaves behind in her wake

Acknowledgements

Earlier versions of "Cabin," "I Love You" and "Oubliette" were published in the anthology, *Crystal Garden/Kristálykert*, 2001

An earlier version of "Weekend" was published in *The Muse Journal*, Volume One, Issue #6, November 1992.

I would like to thank the Canada Council for the Arts and the Ontario Arts Council. I would especially like to thank Michael Mirolla and everyone at Guernica Editions for bringing this book to fruition.

I am grateful for the encouragement, support and friendship from the poets Nik Beat (RIP), John Tarnoc (RIP), Diane Turkosky, Brenda Clews, and especially Brandon Pitts, my first editor.

I am grateful for the support, love, and inspiration I received from my parents, Zalakha and Mubarak, and my daughter, Natasha.

I am especially thankful to my partner, Duane Mac-Neill, for his unending support and love.

About the Author

Jennifer Hosein is a Toronto-based, Montreal-born writer, visual artist, and teacher. Her poems, short fiction, and a play have been published in magazines including *Event* and *Rubicon* and translated into Hungarian for the anthology *Crystal Garden/Kristálykert*. Her artwork has appeared on book covers, in magazines, and in solo and group exhibitions in Toronto.